Uncle Jerry's Great Idea

Norma Shapiro

Name _____

Age _____

Class _____

OXFORD
UNIVERSITY PRESS

OXFORD

UNIVERSITY PRESS

Great Clarendon Street, Oxford OX2 6DP

Oxford University Press is a department of the University of Oxford.
It furthers the University's objective of excellence in research, scholarship,
and education by publishing worldwide in

Oxford New York

Auckland Cape Town Dar es Salaam Hong Kong Karachi
Kuala Lumpur Madrid Melbourne Mexico City Nairobi
New Delhi Shanghai Taipei Toronto

With offices in

Argentina Austria Brazil Chile Czech Republic France Greece
Guatemala Hungary Italy Japan South Korea Poland Portugal
Singapore Switzerland Thailand Turkey Ukraine Vietnam

OXFORD and OXFORD ENGLISH are registered trade marks of
Oxford University Press in the UK and in certain other countries

ISBN: 978 0 19 440102 9

Printed in China

Illustrations by: Andy Hunt
With thanks to Sally Spray for her contribution to this series

📖 Using the book

1 Begin by looking at the first story page (page 2). Look at the picture and ask questions about it. Then read the story text under the picture with your students. Use section 1 of the CD for this if possible.

2 Teach and check the understanding of any new vocabulary. Note that some of the words are in the **Picture Dictionary** at the back of the book.

3 Now look at the activities on the right-hand page. Show the example to the students and instruct them to complete the activities. This may be done individually, in pairs, or as a class.

4 Do the same for the remaining pages of the book.

5 Retell the whole story more quickly, reinforcing the new vocabulary. Section 2 of the CD can help with this.

6 If possible, listen to the expanded story (section 3 of the CD). The students should follow in their books.

7 When the book is finished, use the **Picture Dictionary** to check that students understand and remember new vocabulary. Section 4 of the CD can help with this.

💿 Using the CD

The CD contains four sections.

1 The story told slowly, with pauses. Use this during the first reading. It may also be used for "Listen and repeat" activities at any point.

2 The story told at normal speed. This should be used once the students have read the book for the first time.

3 The expanded story. The story is told in a longer version. This will help the students understand English when it is spoken faster, as they will now know the story and the vocabulary.

4 Vocabulary. Each word in the **Picture Dictionary** is spoken and then used in a simple sentence.

On Saturday Jim's family went to
the park.
His father played baseball. His
mother played tennis. His sister
played basketball. His Uncle Jerry
played baseball, too.

1 Connect.

baseball

bat •

tennis ball •

basketball

hoop •

• racket

2 Complete.

❶ We play basketball with a
   __basketball__ and a _____.

❷ We play tennis with a _____
   and a _____.

❸ We play baseball with a
   _____ and a _____.

3

On Saturday, Jim played baseball, too, but on his computer.

Jim's mother and father were not happy.
"He never goes to the park," his mother said quietly.

Complete. Use these words:

never   sometimes   usually   always

❶ Jim ___always___ stays home on Saturdays.

❷ He _____ reads books.

❸ He _____ plays tennis.

❹ He _____ goes to school on Mondays.

❺ He _____ goes to the park.

❻ He _____ watches TV.

❼ He _____ uses his computer.

❽ He _____ does his homework.

"You always stay home on the
  computer," said his father. "Why
  don't you come to the park?"
"I don't like the park," said Jim,
"I like my computer."
  Now Jim wasn't happy.

Look and write.

He likes		He doesn't like	
home	computer	park	books
pizza	green	rice	pink
soda		coffee	

❶ Jim likes his home but he doesn't like the park.

❷

❸

❹

❺

"I don't like the park," said Jim.

"I have an idea," said Uncle Jerry.

"Next Saturday, bring some paper
and a pencil to the park."

Look at the pictures on page 8 and page 9. Write the six differences.

➊ Jerry _is wearing a hat_ .

➋ Jerry _____ .

➌ Jerry _____ .

➍ The door _____ .

➎ Jim _____ .

➏ Jim _____ .

The next Saturday, Jim went to the
park. His father went up to bat.
"Watch us play and count
    everything we do," said Uncle Jerry.
"OK," said Jim.

Where did Jim go? Write.

Monday	Tuesday	Wednesday
school	the store	math class

Thursday	Friday	Saturday
his friend's house	the movies	the park

❶ On Monday,

he went to school .

❷ On Tuesday,

_____ .

❸ On Wednesday,

_____ .

❹ On Thursday,

_____ .

❺ On Friday,

_____ .

❻ On Saturday,

_____ .

"Is it like baseball on the
   computer?" asked Jim.

"Yes. Just count the times we get runs
   and hits," Uncle Jerry said.

So Jim started to count and write.

Complete.

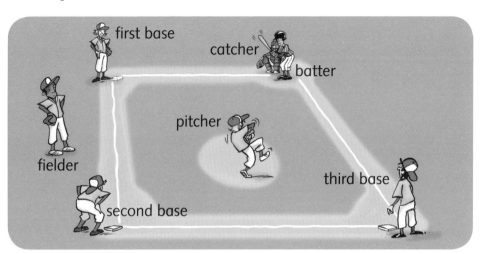

❶ The ___pitcher___ throws the ball.

❷ The _____ hits the ball with the bat.

❸ The _____ stops the ball.

❹ The _____ runs to _____ base, _____ base, and _____ base.

❺ The fielder _____ the ball to the catcher.

❻ The _____ catches the ball.

13

Then Jim's father hit a long
home run!

"Count the home runs, too!" said
Uncle Jerry.

"OK. Great idea," said Jim.

Who else hit a home run? Write.

Tom   Joe   Ben   Sam   Rob

❶ The man who hit the home run
   has long brown hair.

❷ The man who hit the home run
   has glasses.

❸ The man who hit the home run
   has black shoes.

❹ The man who hit the home run
   has a white shirt.

❺ Who hit the home run? _____

After the game they all went home.
Uncle Jerry said to Jim, "Go and
make a chart on your computer."
"OK," said Jim, and he ran up to
his room.

Rewrite the sentences in the past tense.

❶ Jim goes to the park.

Jim went to the park.

❷ Jim watches the game.

_____

❸ Jim counts the runs.

_____

❹ Jim's father hits a home run.

_____

❺ They all go home.

_____

❻ Jim uses his computer.

_____

❼ Jim makes a chart.

_____

This is Jim's chart.

Look at the numbers.

Well done, Jim.

Who made the most runs?

Did Uncle Jerry hit a home run?

Write the answers.

1 Who made the chart?

Jim made the chart.

2 Who made one run?

3 Who made three runs?

4 Who made three hits?

5 Who counted the hits?

6 Who hit a home run?

7 Who made the most runs?

At lunch, Jim gave the chart to his father.

"This is great! I really like it!" said his father. Jim had a big smile on his face.

Rearrange the words.

1 home father a Jim's hit run.

<u>Jim's father hit a home run.</u>

2 home Jim counted runs the.

_____

3 a computer made on chart his Jim.

_____

4 the gave Jim chart his father to.

_____

5 father chart Jim's the liked.

_____

6 smile Jim's had big father a.

_____

7 Jim boy smart is a.

_____

"Can you do one for basketball,
    please?" asked his sister.
"Yes," said Jim.
    Uncle Jerry smiled. Now Jim goes
    to the park every Saturday, and he
    always brings paper and a pencil.

Put the sentences in order.
Number them 1 to 8.

❶ ☐ Jim talked to Uncle Jerry.

❷ ☐ Jim's father hit a home run.

❸ 1 Jim's family went to the park.

❹ ☐ Jim and his family went home.

❺ ☐ Jim started to count the runs.

❻ ☐ Jim made a chart on his computer.

❼ ☐ Jim stayed at home and played on his computer.

❽ ☐ Jim went to the park with paper and a pencil.

Picture Dictionary

baseball

batter

basketball

catcher

bat

chart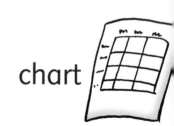

computer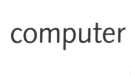

hoop

fielder

pitcher

glasses

racket

hit

smile

Dolphin Readers

Dolphin Readers are available at five levels, from Starter to 4.

The Dolphins series covers four major themes:

Grammar, Living Together, The World Around Us, Science and Nature.

For each theme, there are two titles at every level.

Activity Books are available for all Dolphins.

All Dolphins are available on audio CD.
(2 TITLES ON EACH CD 💿 SEE TABLE BELOW)

Teacher's Notes are available at **www.oup.com/elt/dolphins**

	Grammar	Living Together	The World Around Us	Science and Nature
Starter	• Silly Squirrel • Monkeying Around	• My Family • A Day with Baby	• Doctor, Doctor • Moving House	• A Game of Shapes • Baby Animals
Level 1	• Meet Molly • Where Is It?	• Little Helpers • Jack the Hero	• On Safari • Lost Kitten	• Number Magic • How's the Weather?
Level 2	• Double Trouble • Super Sam	• Candy for Breakfast • Lost!	• A Visit to the City • Matt's Mistake	• Numbers, Numbers Everywhere • Circles and Squares
Level 3	• Students in Space • What Did You Do Yesterday?	• New Girl in School • Uncle Jerry's Great Idea	• Just Like Mine • Wonderful Wild Animals	• Things That Fly • Let's Go to the Rainforest
Level 4	• The Tough Task • Yesterday, Today, and Tomorrow	• We Won the Cup • Up and Down	• Where People Live • City Girl, Country Boy	• In the Ocean • Go, Gorillas, Go